Keep Notes Sis..

Monroe Bishop

MBP

JOURNALS

These Thoughts are mine:
These Experiences are mine:
This Journal is mine:

HEAL,so when someone tells you they love you. You allow yourself to believe them.

_____
_____
_____
_____
_____
_____
_____
_____
_____
_____
_____
_____
_____
_____
_____
_____
_____
_____
_____
_____
_____
_____
_____
_____
_____
_____
_____
_____
_____
_____
_____
_____

Keep Notes Sis..

HEAL,so when someone tells you they love you. You allow yourself to believe them.

_____
_____
_____
_____
_____
_____
_____
_____
_____
_____
_____
_____
_____
_____
_____
_____
_____
_____
_____
_____
_____
_____
_____
_____
_____
_____
_____
_____
_____
_____
_____

Keep Notes Sis..

HEAL, so when someone tells you they love you. You allow yourself to believe them.

Keep Notes Sis..

*HEAL,*so when someone tells you they love you. You allow yourself to believe them.

Keep Notes Sis..

HEAL, so when someone tells you they love you. You allow yourself to believe them.

Keep Notes Sis..

HEAL,so when someone tells you they love you. You allow yourself to believe them.

Keep Notes Sis..

HEAL,so when someone tells you they love you. You allow yourself to believe them.

_____

Keep Notes Sis..

You can find me where I'm Celebrated & Where my love is Reciprocated

_____
_____
_____
_____
_____
_____
_____
_____
_____
_____
_____
_____
_____
_____
_____
_____
_____
_____
_____
_____
_____
_____
_____
_____
_____
_____
_____
_____
_____
_____

Keep Notes Sis..

You can find me where I'm Celebrated & Where my love is Reciprocated

_____
_____
_____
_____
_____
_____
_____
_____
_____
_____
_____
_____
_____
_____
_____
_____
_____
_____
_____
_____
_____
_____
_____
_____
_____
_____
_____
_____
_____
_____
_____
_____

Keep Notes Sis..

You can find me where I'm Celebrated & Where my love is Reciprocated

_____
_____
_____
_____
_____
_____
_____
_____
_____
_____
_____
_____
_____
_____
_____
_____
_____
_____
_____
_____
_____
_____
_____
_____
_____
_____
_____
_____
_____
_____
_____
_____
_____
_____

Keep Notes Sis..

You can find me where I'm Celebrated & Where my love is Reciprocated

_____
_____
_____
_____
_____
_____
_____
_____
_____
_____
_____
_____
_____
_____
_____
_____
_____
_____
_____
_____
_____
_____
_____
_____
_____
_____
_____
_____
_____
_____
_____

Keep Notes Sis..

You can find me where I'm Celebrated & Where my love is Reciprocated

_____
_____
_____
_____
_____
_____
_____
_____
_____
_____
_____
_____
_____
_____
_____
_____
_____
_____
_____
_____
_____
_____
_____
_____
_____
_____
_____
_____
_____
_____
_____
_____
_____
_____

Keep Notes Sis..

You can find me where I'm Celebrated & Where my love is Reciprocated

Keep Notes Sis..

You can find me where I'm Celebrated & Where my love is Reciprocated

_____
_____
_____
_____
_____
_____
_____
_____
_____
_____
_____
_____
_____
_____
_____
_____
_____
_____
_____
_____
_____
_____
_____
_____
_____
_____
_____
_____
_____
_____
_____
_____

Keep Notes Sis..

You are the shit! Stop allowing someone elses dusty ass stress you out!

_____
_____
_____
_____
_____
_____
_____
_____
_____
_____
_____
_____
_____
_____
_____
_____
_____
_____
_____
_____
_____
_____
_____
_____
_____
_____
_____
_____
_____
_____
_____
_____
_____

Keep Notes Sis..

You are the shit! Stop allowing someone elses dusty ass stress you out!

_____
_____
_____
_____
_____
_____
_____
_____
_____
_____
_____
_____
_____
_____
_____
_____
_____
_____
_____
_____
_____
_____
_____
_____
_____
_____
_____
_____
_____
_____
_____
_____

Keep Notes Sis..

You are the shit! Stop allowing someone elses dusty ass stress you out!

Keep Notes Sis..

You are the shit! Stop allowing someone elses dusty ass stress you out!

_____
_____
_____
_____
_____
_____
_____
_____
_____
_____
_____
_____
_____
_____
_____
_____
_____
_____
_____
_____
_____
_____
_____
_____
_____
_____
_____
_____
_____
_____
_____
_____

Keep Notes Sis..

You are the shit! Stop allowing someone elses dusty ass stress you out!

_____
_____
_____
_____
_____
_____
_____
_____
_____
_____
_____
_____
_____
_____
_____
_____
_____
_____
_____
_____
_____
_____
_____
_____
_____
_____
_____
_____
_____
_____
_____

Keep Notes Sis..

You are the shit! Stop allowing someone elses dusty ass stress you out!

_____
_____
_____
_____
_____
_____
_____
_____
_____
_____
_____
_____
_____
_____
_____
_____
_____
_____
_____
_____
_____
_____
_____
_____
_____
_____
_____
_____
_____
_____
_____
_____

Keep Notes Sis..

You are the shit! Stop allowing someone elses dusty ass stress you out!

_____
_____
_____
_____
_____
_____
_____
_____
_____
_____
_____
_____
_____
_____
_____
_____
_____
_____
_____
_____
_____
_____
_____
_____
_____
_____
_____
_____
_____
_____
_____
_____
_____

Keep Notes Sis..

Settling Will Never Feel Right When You Know You Were Meant For More.

Keep Notes Sis..

Settling Will Never Feel Right When You Know You Were Meant For More.

_____
_____
_____
_____
_____
_____
_____
_____
_____
_____
_____
_____
_____
_____
_____
_____
_____
_____
_____
_____
_____
_____
_____
_____
_____
_____
_____
_____
_____
_____
_____
_____
_____

Keep Notes Sis..

Settling Will Never Feel Right When You Know You Were Meant For More.

_____

_____
_____
_____
_____
_____
_____
_____
_____
_____
_____
_____
_____
_____
_____
_____
_____
_____
_____
_____
_____
_____
_____
_____
_____
_____
_____
_____
_____
_____
_____
_____
_____
_____
_____

Keep Notes Sis..

Settling Will Never Feel Right When You Know You Were Meant For More.

Keep Notes Sis..

Settling Will Never Feel Right When You Know You Were Meant For More.

Settling Will Never Feel Right When You Know You Were Meant For More.

Keep Notes Sis..

Settling Will Never Feel Right When You Know You Were Meant For More.

Keep Notes Sis..

You Better Learn a muh'Fker, Before you Love a muh'Fker or your ass gonna be learning a muh'Fking hard lesson

Keep Notes Sis..

You Better Learn a muh'Fker, Before you Love a muh'Fker or your ass gonna be learning a muh'Fking hard lesson

_____
_____
_____
_____
_____
_____
_____
_____
_____
_____
_____
_____
_____
_____
_____
_____
_____
_____
_____
_____
_____
_____
_____
_____
_____
_____
_____
_____
_____
_____
_____
_____
_____
_____

Keep Notes Sis..

You Better Learn a muh'Fker, Before you Love a muh'Fker or your ass gonna be learning a muh'Fking hard lesson

_____
_____
_____
_____
_____
_____
_____
_____
_____
_____
_____
_____
_____
_____
_____
_____
_____
_____
_____
_____
_____
_____
_____
_____
_____
_____
_____
_____
_____
_____
_____
_____
_____

Keep Notes Sis..

You Better Learn a muh'Fker, Before you Love a muh'Fker or your ass gonna be learning a muh'Fking hard lesson

Keep Notes Sis..

You Better Learn a muh'Fker, Before you Love a muh'Fker or your ass gonna be learning a muh'Fking hard lesson

Keep Notes Sis..

You Better Learn a muh'FKer, Before you Love a muh'FKer or your ass gonna be learning a muh'Fking hard lesson

Keep Notes Sis..

You Better Learn a muh'Fker, Before you Love a muh'Fker or your ass gonna be learning a muh'Fking hard lesson

Keep Notes Sis..

Life hits different when you allow yourself to heal.

_____
_____
_____
_____
_____
_____
_____
_____
_____
_____
_____
_____
_____
_____
_____
_____
_____
_____
_____
_____
_____
_____
_____
_____
_____
_____
_____
_____
_____
_____
_____
_____

Keep Notes Sis..

Life hits different when you allow yourself to heal.

_____
_____
_____
_____
_____
_____
_____
_____
_____
_____
_____
_____
_____
_____
_____
_____
_____
_____
_____
_____
_____
_____
_____
_____
_____
_____
_____
_____
_____
_____
_____
_____
_____

Keep Notes Sis..

Life hits different when you allow yourself to heal.

_____
_____
_____
_____
_____
_____
_____
_____
_____
_____
_____
_____
_____
_____
_____
_____
_____
_____
_____
_____
_____
_____
_____
_____
_____
_____
_____
_____
_____
_____

Keep Notes Sis..

Life hits different when you allow yourself to heal.

Keep Notes Sis..

Life hits different when you allow yourself to heal.

Life hits different when you allow yourself to heal.

_____
_____
_____
_____
_____
_____
_____
_____
_____
_____
_____
_____
_____
_____
_____
_____
_____
_____
_____
_____
_____
_____
_____
_____
_____
_____
_____
_____
_____
_____
_____

Keep Notes Sis..

Life hits different when you allow yourself to heal.

_____
_____
_____
_____
_____
_____
_____
_____
_____
_____
_____
_____
_____
_____
_____
_____
_____
_____
_____
_____
_____
_____
_____
_____
_____
_____
_____
_____
_____
_____
_____
_____
_____
_____

Keep Notes Sis..

There is a big difference between accepting someones flaws and accepting someones bullshit

_____
_____
_____
_____
_____
_____
_____
_____
_____
_____
_____
_____
_____
_____
_____
_____
_____
_____
_____
_____
_____
_____
_____
_____
_____
_____
_____
_____
_____
_____

Keep Notes Sis..

There is a big difference between accepting someones flaws and accepting someones bullshit

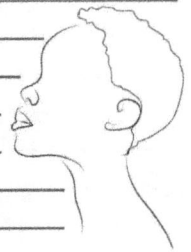

Keep Notes Sis..

There is a big difference between accepting someones flaws and accepting someones bullshit

Keep Notes Sis..

There is a big difference between accepting someones flaws and accepting someones bullshit

_____
_____
_____
_____
_____
_____
_____
_____
_____
_____
_____
_____
_____
_____
_____
_____
_____
_____
_____
_____
_____
_____
_____
_____
_____
_____
_____
_____
_____
_____
_____

Keep Notes Sis..

There is a big difference between accepting someones flaws and accepting someones bullshit

_____
_____
_____
_____
_____
_____
_____
_____
_____
_____
_____
_____
_____
_____
_____
_____
_____
_____
_____
_____
_____
_____
_____
_____
_____
_____
_____
_____
_____
_____
_____

Keep Notes Sis..

There is a big difference between accepting someones flaws and accepting someones bullshit

Keep Notes Sis..

There is a big difference between accepting someones flaws and accepting someones bullshit

Keep Notes Sis..

Everyone is not qualified to love you

_____
_____
_____
_____
_____
_____
_____
_____
_____
_____
_____
_____
_____
_____
_____
_____
_____
_____
_____
_____
_____
_____
_____
_____
_____
_____
_____
_____
_____
_____
_____

Keep Notes Sis..

Everyone is not qualified to love you

Keep Notes Sis..

Everyone is not qualified to love you

_____
_____
_____
_____
_____
_____
_____
_____
_____
_____
_____
_____
_____
_____
_____
_____
_____
_____
_____
_____
_____
_____
_____
_____
_____
_____
_____
_____
_____
_____
_____

Keep Notes Sis..

Everyone is not qualified to love you

Keep Notes Sis..

Everyone is not qualified to love you

_____
_____
_____
_____
_____
_____
_____
_____
_____
_____
_____
_____
_____
_____
_____
_____
_____
_____
_____
_____
_____
_____
_____
_____
_____
_____
_____
_____
_____
_____
_____

Keep Notes Sis..

Everyone is not qualified to love you

_____

Keep Notes Sis..

Everyone is not qualified to love you

Keep Notes Sis..

Never accept anything less than you deserve. Remember you teach people how to treat you.

Keep Notes Sis..

Never accept anything less than you deserve. Remember you teach people how to treat you.

Keep Notes Sis..

Never accept anything less than you deserve. Remember you teach people how to treat you.

Never accept anything less than you deserve. Remember you teach people how to treat you.

Keep Notes Sis..

Never accept anything less than you deserve. Remember you teach people how to treat you.

_____
_____
_____
_____
_____
_____
_____
_____
_____
_____
_____
_____
_____
_____
_____
_____
_____
_____
_____
_____
_____
_____
_____
_____
_____
_____
_____
_____
_____
_____
_____

Keep Notes Sis..

Never accept anything less than you deserve. Remember you teach people how to treat you.

Keep Notes Sis..

Never accept anything less than you deserve. Remember you teach people how to treat you.

Stop holding onto people just because you have a history together

Keep Notes Sis..

Stop holding onto people just because you have a history together

Keep Notes Sis..

Stop holding onto people just because you have a history together

Keep Notes Sis..

Stop holding onto people just because you have a history together

_____
_____
_____
_____
_____
_____
_____
_____
_____
_____
_____
_____
_____
_____
_____
_____
_____
_____
_____
_____
_____
_____
_____
_____
_____
_____
_____
_____
_____

Keep Notes Sis..

Stop holding onto people just because you have a history together

Keep Notes Sis..

Stop holding onto people just because you have a history together

Keep Notes Sis..

Stop holding onto people just because you have a history together

Keep Notes Sis..

sometimes the healing hurts more than the wound

Keep Notes Sis..

sometimes the healing hurts more than the wound

Keep Notes Sis..

sometimes the healing hurts more than the wound

Keep Notes Sis..

sometimes the healing hurts more than the wound

Keep Notes Sis..

sometimes the healing hurts more than the wound

Keep Notes Sis..

sometimes the healing hurts more than the wound

Keep Notes Sis..

sometimes the healing hurts more than the wound

Keep Notes Sis..

Don't Be A Victim

Keep Notes Sis..

Don't Be A Victim

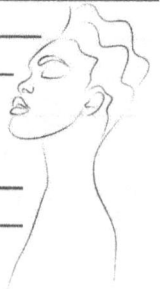

Keep Notes Sis..

Don't Be A Victim

Keep Notes Sis..

Don't Be A Victim

Don't Be A Victim

Keep Notes Sis..

Don't Be A Victim

Don't Be A Victim

Keep Notes Sis..

Your Value Doesn't decrease based on someones inability to see your worth

Keep Notes Sis..

Your Value Doesn't decrease based on someones inability to see your worth

Keep Notes Sis..

Your Value Doesn't decrease based on someones inability to see your worth

Keep Notes Sis..

Your Value Doesn't decrease based on someones inability to see your worth

Keep Notes Sis..

Your Value Doesn't decrease based on someones inability to see your worth

Your Value Doesn't decrease based on someones inability to see your worth

_____
_____
_____
_____
_____
_____
_____
_____
_____
_____
_____
_____
_____
_____
_____
_____
_____
_____
_____
_____
_____
_____
_____
_____
_____
_____
_____
_____
_____
_____
_____
_____

Keep Notes Sis..

Your Value Doesn't decrease based on someones inability to see your worth

I used to Think I can save everyone, until I realized they were drowning me

Keep Notes Sis..

I used to Think I can save everyone, until I realized they were drowning me

_____
_____
_____
_____
_____
_____
_____
_____
_____
_____
_____
_____
_____
_____
_____
_____
_____
_____
_____
_____
_____
_____
_____
_____
_____
_____
_____
_____
_____
_____

Keep Notes Sis..

I used to Think I can save everyone, until I realized they were drowning me

Keep Notes Sis..

I used to Think I can save everyone, until I realized they were drowning me

Keep Notes Sis..

I used to Think I can save everyone, until I realized they were drowning me

Keep Notes Sis..

I used to Think I can save everyone, until I realized they were drowning me

_____
_____
_____
_____
_____
_____
_____
_____
_____
_____
_____
_____
_____
_____
_____
_____
_____
_____
_____
_____
_____
_____
_____
_____
_____
_____
_____
_____
_____
_____
_____
_____

Keep Notes Sis..

GIRL, Do it for you

Keep Notes Sis..

GIRL, Do it For you

Keep Notes Sis..

GIRL, Do it For you

Keep Notes Sis..

GIRL, Do it for you

Keep Notes Sis..

GIRL, Do it For you

_____
_____
_____
_____
_____
_____
_____
_____
_____
_____
_____
_____
_____
_____
_____
_____
_____
_____
_____
_____
_____
_____
_____
_____
_____
_____
_____
_____
_____
_____
_____
_____

Keep Notes Sis..

GIRL, Do it for you

Keep Notes Sis..

GIRL, Do it For you

Keep Notes Sis..

"You have to cherish things in a different way when you know the clock is ticking" ~ Chadwick Boseman

Keep Notes Sis..

"You have to cherish things in a different way when you know the clock is ticking" ~ Chadwick Boseman

Keep Notes Sis..

"You have to cherish things in a different way when you know the clock is ticking"~ Chadwick Boseman

Keep Notes Sis..

"You have to cherish things in a different way when you know the clock is ticking" ~ Chadwick Boseman

Keep Notes Sis..

"You have to cherish things in a different way when you know the clock is ticking" ~ Chadwick Boseman

_____
_____
_____
_____
_____
_____
_____
_____
_____
_____
_____
_____
_____
_____
_____
_____
_____
_____
_____
_____
_____
_____
_____
_____
_____
_____
_____
_____
_____
_____
_____
_____

Keep Notes Sis..

'You have to cherish things in a different way when you know the clock is ticking' ~ Chadwick Boseman

Keep Notes Sis..

"You have to cherish things in a different way when you know the clock is ticking"~ Chadwick Boseman

Keep Notes Sis..

They say you'll keep forgving someone you love until you hate them.

Keep Notes Sis..

They say you'll keep Forgving someone you love until you hate them.

Keep Notes Sis..

They say you'll keep Forgving someone you love until you hate them.

Keep Notes Sis..

They say you'll keep Forgving someone you love until you hate them.

_____
_____
_____
_____
_____
_____
_____
_____
_____
_____
_____
_____
_____
_____
_____
_____
_____
_____
_____
_____
_____
_____
_____
_____
_____
_____
_____
_____
_____
_____

Keep Notes Sis..

They say you'll keep forgiving someone you love until you hate them.

Keep Notes Sis..

They say you'll keep Forgving someone you love until you hate them.

Keep Notes Sis..

They say you'll keep forgiving someone you love until you hate them.

Keep Notes Sis..

Not everyone will grow with you.

Keep Notes Sis..

Not everyone will grow with you.

_____
_____
_____
_____
_____
_____
_____
_____
_____
_____
_____
_____
_____
_____
_____
_____
_____
_____
_____
_____
_____
_____
_____
_____
_____
_____
_____
_____
_____
_____
_____
_____

Keep Notes Sis..

Not everyone will grow with you.

_____
_____
_____
_____
_____
_____
_____
_____
_____
_____
_____
_____
_____
_____
_____
_____
_____
_____
_____
_____
_____
_____
_____
_____
_____
_____
_____
_____
_____
_____

Keep Notes Sis..

Not everyone will grow with you.

_____

_____

_____

_____

_____

_____

_____

_____

_____

_____

_____

_____

_____

_____

_____

_____

_____

_____

_____

_____

_____

_____

_____

_____

_____

Keep Notes Sis..

Not everyone will grow with you.

Keep Notes Sis..

Not everyone will grow with you.

Keep Notes Sis..

Not everyone will grow with you.

Keep Notes Sis..

it takes grace to remain kind in cruel situations

Keep Notes Sis..

it takes grace to remain kind in cruel situations

_____
_____
_____
_____
_____
_____
_____
_____
_____
_____
_____
_____
_____
_____
_____
_____
_____
_____
_____
_____
_____
_____
_____
_____
_____
_____
_____
_____

Keep Notes Sis..

it takes grace to remain kind in cruel situations

Keep Notes Sis..

it takes grace to remain kind in cruel situations

Keep Notes Sis..

it takes grace to remain kind in cruel situations

Keep Notes Sis..

it takes grace to remain kind in cruel situations

_____
_____
_____
_____
_____
_____
_____
_____
_____
_____
_____
_____
_____
_____
_____
_____
_____
_____
_____
_____
_____
_____
_____
_____
_____
_____
_____
_____
_____
_____
_____

Keep Notes Sis..

it takes grace to remain kind in cruel situations

Keep Notes Sis..

Chin Up Bitch! .. You Got this!

Keep Notes Sis..

Chin Up Bitch! .. You Got this!

Keep Notes Sis..

Chin Up Bitch! .. You Got this!

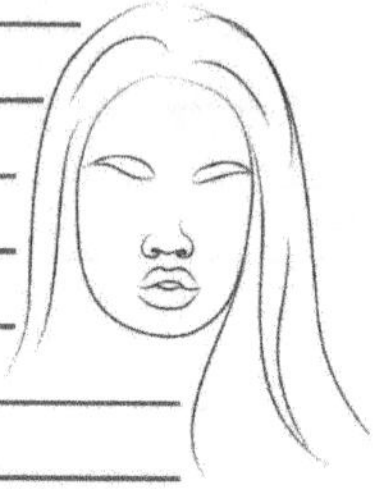

Keep Notes Sis..

Chin Up Bitch! .. You Got this!

Chin Up Bitch! .. You Got this!

Chin Up Bitch! .. You Got this!

Chin Up Bitch! ..You Got this!

Keep Notes Sis..

Biggest flex is loving yourself, so Dont Give up on Love.

_____
_____
_____
_____
_____
_____
_____
_____
_____
_____
_____
_____
_____
_____
_____
_____
_____
_____
_____
_____
_____
_____
_____
_____
_____
_____
_____
_____

Keep Notes Sis..

Biggest flex is loving yourself, so Dont Give up on Love.

_____
_____
_____
_____
_____
_____
_____
_____
_____
_____
_____
_____
_____
_____
_____
_____
_____
_____
_____
_____
_____
_____
_____
_____
_____
_____
_____
_____
_____
_____
_____
_____

Keep Notes Sis..

Biggest flex is loving yourself, so Dont Give up on Love.

Keep Notes Sis..

Biggest flex is loving yourself, so Dont Give up on Love.

Keep Notes Sis..

Biggest flex is loving yourself, so Don't Give up on Love.

Keep Notes Sis..

Biggest flex is loving yourself, so Dont Give up on Love.

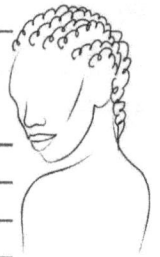

_____
_____
_____
_____
_____
_____
_____
_____
_____
_____
_____
_____
_____
_____
_____
_____
_____
_____
_____
_____
_____
_____
_____
_____
_____
_____
_____
_____
_____
_____
_____

Keep Notes Sis..

Biggest flex is loving yourself, so Don't Give up on Love.

_____
_____
_____
_____
_____
_____
_____
_____
_____
_____
_____
_____
_____
_____
_____
_____
_____
_____
_____
_____
_____
_____
_____
_____
_____
_____
_____
_____
_____
_____

Keep Notes Sis..

Life is too short to be on some Unhappy shit!!!

Keep Notes Sis..

Life is too short to be on some Unhappy shit!!!

Keep Notes Sis..

Life is too short to be on some Unhappy shit!!!

Keep Notes Sis..

Life is too short to be on some Unhappy shit!!!

Keep Notes Sis..

Life is too short to be on some Unhappy shit!!!

Keep Notes Sis..

Life is too short to be on some Unhappy shit!!!

Keep Notes Sis..

Life is too short to be on some Unhappy shit!!!

_____
_____
_____
_____
_____
_____
_____
_____
_____
_____
_____
_____
_____
_____
_____
_____
_____
_____
_____
_____
_____
_____
_____
_____
_____
_____
_____
_____
_____
_____
_____
_____
_____

Keep Notes Sis..

"Be the girl who knows her peace is her responsibility"

Keep Notes Sis..

"Be the girl who knows her peace is her responsibility"

Keep Notes Sis..

"Be the girl who knows her peace is her responsibility"

Keep Notes Sis..

"Be the girl who knows her peace is her responsibility"

Keep Notes Sis..

"Be the girl who knows her peace is her responsibility"

_____
_____
_____
_____
_____
_____
_____
_____
_____
_____
_____
_____
_____
_____
_____
_____
_____
_____
_____
_____
_____
_____
_____
_____
_____
_____
_____
_____
_____
_____
_____

Keep Notes Sis..

"Be the girl who knows her peace is her responsibility"

Keep Notes Sis..

"Be the girl who knows her peace is her responsibility"

Keep Notes Sis..

"Just because you carry it well doesn't mean its not heavy"

Keep Notes Sis..

"Just because you carry it well doesn't mean its not heavy"

Keep Notes Sis..

"Just because you carry it well doesn't mean its not heavy"

Keep Notes Sis..

"Just because you carry it well doesnt mean its not heavy"

Keep Notes Sis..

"Just because you carry it well doesnt mean its not heavy"

Keep Notes Sis..

"Just because you carry it well doesn't mean its not heavy"

Keep Notes Sis..

"Just because you carry it well doesnt mean its not heavy"

Keep Notes Sis..

"A fresh start isn't a new place, its a mindset."

Keep Notes Sis..

"A fresh start isn't a new place, its a mindset."

Keep Notes Sis..

"A fresh start isn't a new place, it's a mindset."

Keep Notes Sis..

"A fresh start isn't a new place, it's a mindset."

"A fresh start isn't a new place, it's a mindset."

"A fresh start isn't a new place, it's a mindset."

Keep Notes Sis..

"A fresh start isn't a new place, its a mindset."

Keep Notes Sis..

When it doesn't bother you like it use to, baby that's healing.

_____
_____
_____
_____
_____
_____
_____
_____
_____
_____
_____
_____
_____
_____
_____
_____
_____
_____
_____
_____
_____
_____
_____
_____
_____
_____
_____
_____
_____
_____

Keep Notes Sis..

When it doesn't bother you like it use to, baby that's healing.

Keep Notes Sis..

When it doesn't bother you like it use to, baby that's healing.

_____
_____
_____
_____
_____
_____
_____
_____
_____
_____
_____
_____
_____
_____
_____
_____
_____
_____
_____
_____
_____
_____
_____
_____
_____
_____
_____
_____
_____
_____

Keep Notes Sis..

When it doesn't bother you like it use to, baby that's healing.

_____
_____
_____
_____
_____
_____
_____
_____
_____
_____
_____
_____
_____
_____
_____
_____
_____
_____
_____
_____
_____
_____
_____
_____
_____
_____
_____
_____
_____

Keep Notes Sis..

When it doesn't bother you like it use to, baby that's healing.

Keep Notes Sis..

When it doesn't bother you like it use to, baby that's healing.

_____
_____
_____
_____
_____
_____
_____
_____
_____
_____
_____
_____
_____
_____
_____
_____
_____
_____
_____
_____
_____
_____
_____
_____
_____
_____
_____
_____
_____
_____
_____

Keep Notes Sis..

When it doesn't bother you like it use to, baby that's healing.

Keep Notes Sis..

"Loving Yourself Is Not Vanity It Is Sanity"

Keep Notes Sis..

"Loving Yourself Is Not Vanity It Is Sanity"

Keep Notes Sis..

"Loving Yourself Is Not Vanity It Is Sanity"

_____
_____
_____
_____
_____
_____
_____
_____
_____
_____
_____
_____
_____
_____
_____
_____
_____
_____
_____
_____
_____
_____
_____
_____
_____
_____
_____
_____
_____
_____
_____
_____

Keep Notes Sis..

"Loving Yourself Is Not Vanity It Is Sanity"

Keep Notes Sis..

"Loving Yourself Is Not Vanity It Is Sanity"

Keep Notes Sis..

Don't let anyone bullshit you, healing is fucking difficult ~Unknown

_____
_____
_____
_____
_____
_____
_____
_____
_____
_____
_____
_____
_____
_____
_____
_____
_____
_____
_____
_____
_____
_____
_____
_____
_____
_____
_____
_____
_____
_____
_____
_____

Don't let anyone bullshit you, healing is fucking difficult ~Unknown

Don't let anyone bullshit you, healing is fucking difficult ~Unknown

Don't let anyone bullshit you, healing is fucking difficult ~Unknown

Don't let anyone bullshit you, healing is fucking difficult ~Unknown

Don't let anyone bullshit you, healing is fucking difficult ~Unknown

Don't let anyone bullshit you, healing is fucking difficult ~Unknown

_____
_____
_____
_____
_____
_____
_____
_____
_____
_____
_____
_____
_____
_____
_____
_____
_____
_____
_____
_____
_____
_____
_____
_____
_____
_____
_____
_____
_____
_____
_____
_____

Don't let anyone bullshit you, healing is fucking difficult ~Unknown

When you start seeing your worth,
you'll find it harder
to stay around people who don't